Party every day,
sing and jump about.
Everybody shout...

CBeebies House!

It's playtime!

Try these puzzles with Bing and his friends.

Everyone has **chosen a toy!**

I'll make you better, Hoppity!

I'm a fairy queen!

I love Bullabaloo!

Who's holding the **fairy wand?**

Bing   Sula   Pando

They're all in a line!

✓ Tick which **toy comes next** for Pando!

Who's inside?

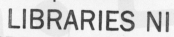

5

♪ Let's sing! ♪

Write, colour and sing with the CBeebies House friends.

Bing and Sula are **sharing balloons!**

How many balloons **altogether?**

There are more blue orange balloons!

Help Bing **finish his picture!**

It's a picture of me!

Open water

Meet a lion's mane jellyfish with the Octonauts!

Wow, look at those tentacles!

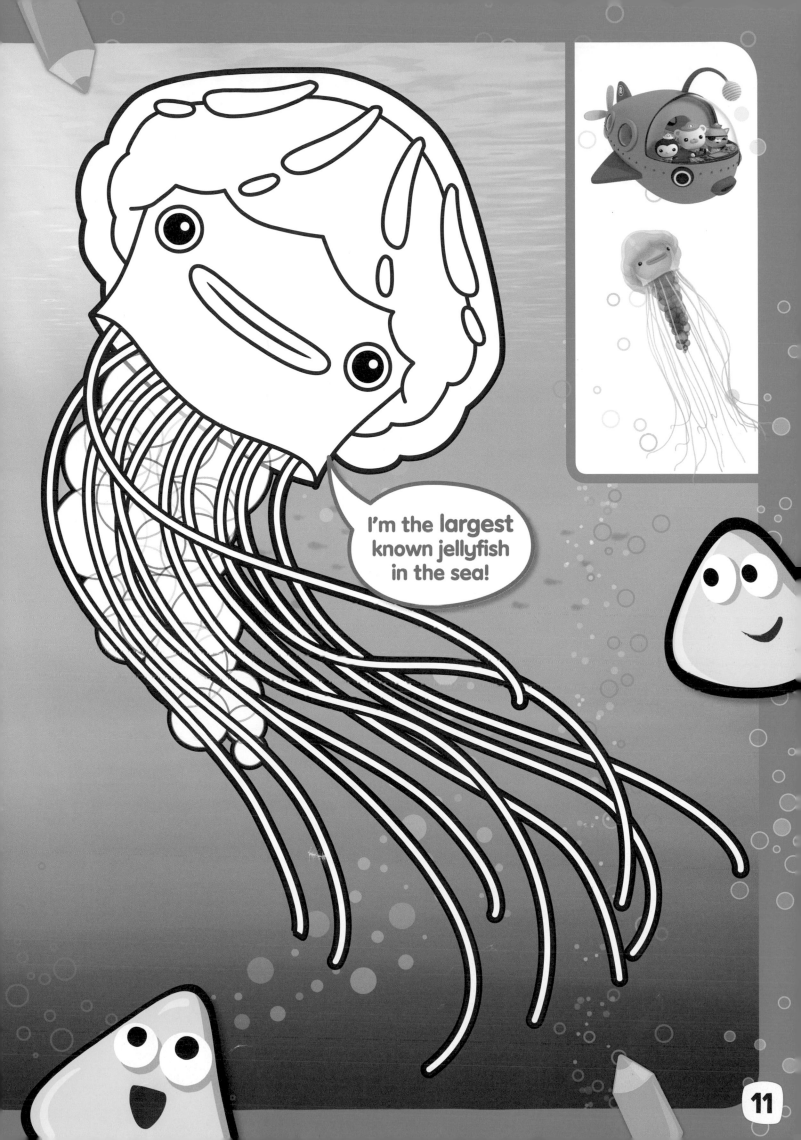

Dino trail

Join Andy on an amazing adventure!

Let's race back to the clock!

Draw a path to lead Andy past the dinosaurs!

Fact!
Allosaurus had strong legs that made it a fast runner.

Fact!
Triceratops used its large horns to defend itself.

Fact!
Tyrannosaurus Rex had 60 sharp teeth. Each was as big as a banana!

ROAR!

Colour the magic clock!

Fact!
Diplodocus was 26 metres long! It could reach high into the trees to chomp leaves.

Fact!
Stegosaurus had spiky plates of bone along its back!

YOU DID IT!
Colour a claw.

Puppies

Meet this furry friend.

Choose a name for this puppy.

....

Pupp[ies] need lot[s of] **love an[d] attentio[n]**

Puppies need a cosy, safe place to **sleep and rest.**

Woof!

Food helps puppies to grow.

Pets need **lots of water** to drink.

14

Kittens

Find out about baby cats.

Kittens like gentle stroking. Give this kitten a gentle stroke.

Miaow!

Choose a name for this kitten.

....

Kittens **love to climb up high!**

They need lots of **fun toys to play with.**

They're so cuddly!

Fun in Numberland

It's time for some number fun!

I'm Number One and this is fun!

One sunny day, One was walking in Numberland. "I am One. This is fun!" she giggled, twirling around. One pointed to the black number 1 above her head. "This is my numberling. It means One. ME!" she said. One did a little skip and looked around. "This is one wonderful world!" she laughed.

1 bird and 1 tree!

One looked up. She spotted a bird. "1 bird!" she laughed. Then she spotted a tree. "1 tree!" she pointed. "1 wonderful world, and 1 ME!" she sang.

One walked a bit more. "But it's a bit lonely, being the only One," she thought. So she went to find Two. He was marching around. "1, 2, 1, 2," he sang as he marched. "I love things there are 2 of," Two said. "Look! 2 dancing shoes," he smiled, clicking his feet together. "Brilliant!" laughed One, as Two danced.

Now there are 2 of us!

"These shoes belong together, like friends," smiled Two. So the 2 friends had some fun. First, they kicked a football together. Next, they played hide-and-seek. Then, they rode a tandem bike. "Everything is better with 2," laughed Two.

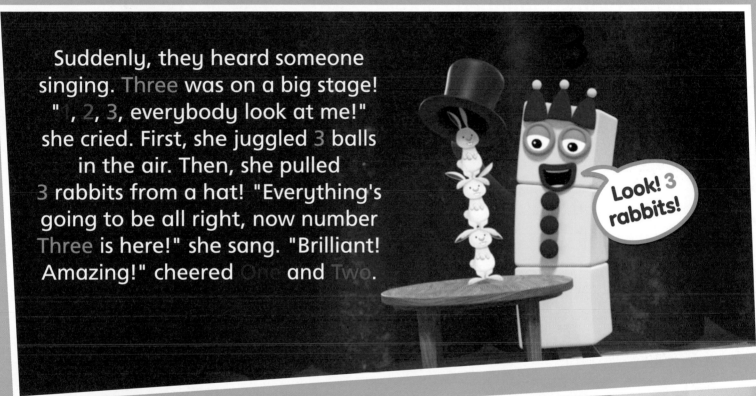

Suddenly, they heard someone singing. Three was on a big stage! "1, 2, 3, everybody look at me!" she cried. First, she juggled 3 balls in the air. Then, she pulled 3 rabbits from a hat! "Everything's going to be all right, now number Three is here!" she sang. "Brilliant! Amazing!" cheered One and Two.

Look! 3 rabbits!

I'm Four. I love to be square!

Next, One, Two and Three decided to go and see Four. They knocked at the door. "Hello! Come in," said Four. His house was very square! There was a square lamp and a square chair, and a square table too!

Four even had a square pet, called Squarey! "I love to be square! A square has 4 sides and 4 corners," said Four. Just then, Four noticed something. "Someone's nibbled 4 holes in my tablecloth!" It was Squarey! "You cheeky little square. How can we fix this?" Four laughed. Squarey scampered behind the kitchen cupboard, and carried 4 plates to the table, covering each hole. "Perfect! 4 plates!" laughed Four.

"Now, who wants a square cookie?" asked Four. "Yes please!" cheered One, Two and Three. Four ran over to the cookie jar, but it was on a very high shelf. Four couldn't reach! "We need some help," he said. Just then, there was a knock on the door. It was Five!

"I am Five. I feel alive!" said Five. "You're just in time. I can't reach the cookie jar!" said Four. "I'm one block more than you, so I can reach," smiled Five, stretching up to get the jar. "Hooray!" the Numberblocks cheered. "Now that's done, I think it's time for some music," said Five. So the Numberblocks hopped into Five's motor car. It had 5 seats!

I'm 5 blocks tall!

Five drove to the big stage. "Time for a star turn!" she smiled, handing out instruments. "Brilliant!" cheered the Numberblocks. "I LOVE stars! They have 5 points, which makes me a ROCK STAR!" said Five. The band started to play.

"5 members in my band, 5 fingers on my hand, 5 points on a shooting star, 5 seats in my motor car!" sang Five.

"1, 2, 3, 4, 5," sang the Numberblocks. "You know that you've arrived when you're with number Five," laughed Five. What a day!

The end

Click-Ons

Colour the picture to get the
Go Jetters ready for action!

G.O. FIX

G.O. GRAB

20

G.O. BOOTS

G.O. ROLL

Funny puzzles

Trace, colour and giggle!

Wizard Tripwick can make rubber ducks appear out of thin air!

Prepare to be ASTOUNDED!

How many rubber ducks can you count?

Draw the adora-beam to zap **Captain Adorable's** stinky socks!

I'll defeat you, stinky socks!

Who am I?

Use the clues to guess the animals.

Can you guess?

I have **green** and slimy skin.

I have a **long tongue** for catching flies.

I am **black** and **white**.

I eat **grass.**

I am **pink** with a snout.

I like **rolling in mud.**

Great work!

I have **brown** fur.

I wear special **shoes.**

Use these pictures to help.

horse

cow   frog   pig

I say   I am a...

ribbit!   ....

I say   I am a...

moo!   ....

I say   I am a...

oink!   ....

I say   I am a...

neigh!   ....

25

Ball!

Draw, colour and write to learn a new word with Dee.

Gem's jewels

Add lots of colour to this pirate picture.

Stick dance

Learn these moves and dance along
with Duggee and the Squirrels.

Stick, stick, stick, stick, stick, stick, stick, stick, stick, stick, stick, stick.   Sticky, sticky, stick, stick!

Jump up and down 12 times...   then wiggle, wiggle, hop, hop!

Stick, stick, stick, stick, stick, stick, stick, stick, stick, stick, stick, stick.   Sticky, sticky, stick, stick!

Stamp 6 times to the right, then 6 times to the left... then wiggle, wiggle, hop, hop!

Stick, stick, stick, stick, stick, stick, stick, stick, stick, stick, stick, stick.   Sticky, sticky, stick, stick!

Now rave! Punch up right 6 times, punch up left 6 times...   STOP! Now freeze!

Stick, stick, stick, stick, stick, stick, stick, stick, stick, stick, stick, stick.   Sticky, sticky, stick, stick!

CLAP!

CLAP!   CLAP!   CLAP!   CLAP!

Clap your hands 12 times!   Then wiggle, wiggle, hop, hop!

Colour Duggee's body paint!

WOOOOOF!

STICK!

29

Doctor Doodles

Draw some lovely pictures for Dr Ranj's waiting room.

You could draw...

Use lots of colour!

They look great!

Spot the bugs

Tick off the bugs when you see them.

Can you find them all?

Excellent spotting!

33

Wordplay

Search, tick and write to finish these Alphablocks puzzles.

a	l	o	g
b	e	e	a
u	n	e	n
g	p	n	t

I wonder where the words are?

bug

ant

log

bee

Fill in the words using the pictures to help.

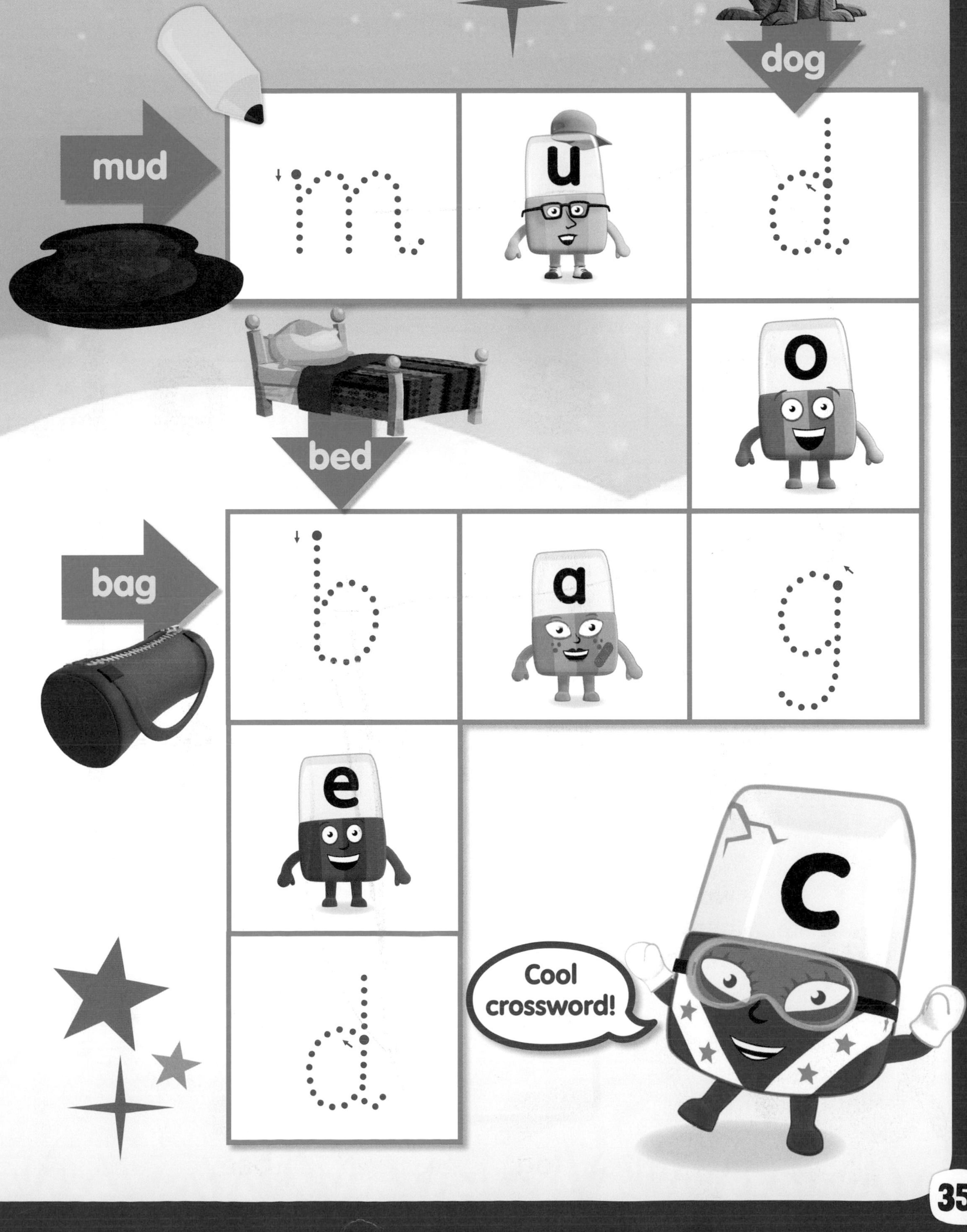

dog

mud

m. u d

bed

o

bag

b a g

e

d

Cool crossword!

c

All about bugs!

Help Topsy and Tim find out about these little critters.

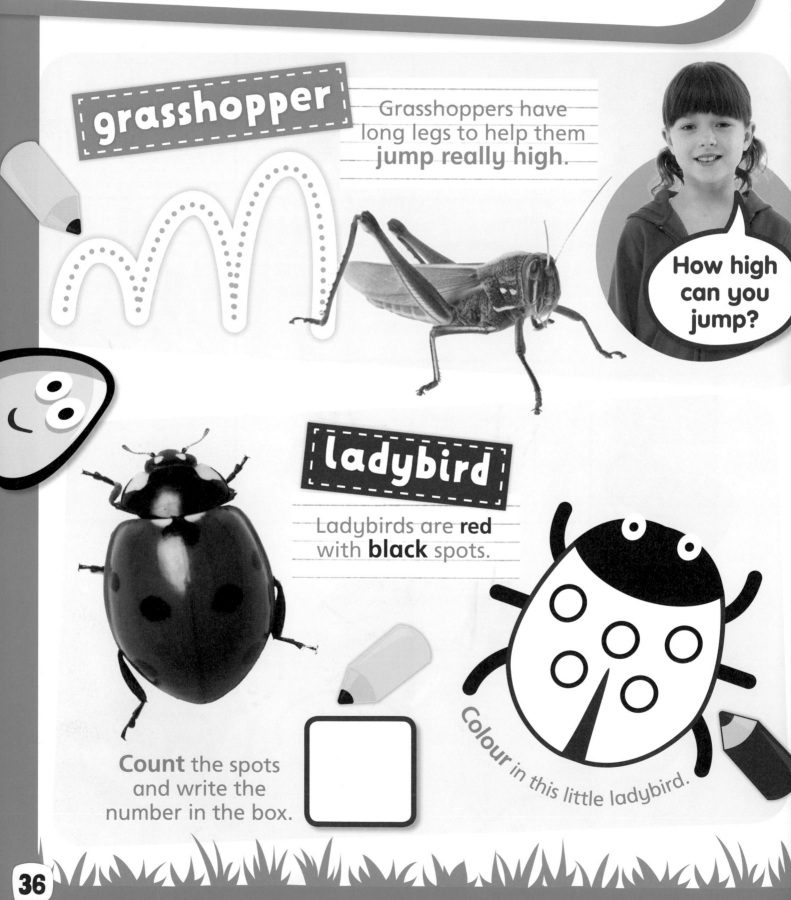

grasshopper

Grasshoppers have long legs to help them **jump really high.**

How high can you jump?

ladybird

Ladybirds are **red** with **black** spots.

Count the spots and write the number in the box.

Colour in this little ladybird.

caterpillar

Caterpillars eat **lots of leaves.**

Draw some leaves for the hungry caterpillar to munch on.

cocoon

Then they **wrap themselves up** in a cocoon.

After a few days, they turn into a beautiful...

butterfly

Colour this butterfly's wing.

Can you flutter like a butterfly?

Butterflies' wings are **exactly the same** on both sides.

Colouring fun!

Waffle game

Find a friend and race to the finish!

Start!

Pop your **counters** here.

1

2

3 Chase a buzzy bee to **space 5!**

4

5

14

21

20

19
Dance with Simon to **space 21!**

15 Chase after a ball to **space 17.**

22

18

16

17

No running!

40

How to play

1 Find a **dice,** and use coins for **counters.** Pretend the coins are Waffle and George.

2 Take it in turns to **roll** the dice and **move** around the board.

3 The first person to reach the finish is the **winner!**

6 Miss a go to dig up the flower bed.

7

8 Secret tunnel! Go to **space** 12.

How are you feeling today?

9

How did you get through there?

10 Go back to 9 for a vet check-up with Jess.

13 Race back **to 11** with Mrs Hobbs' slippers!

12

11

Finish!

23 Treat time! Run to space 24.

Who's hungry?

25

24

Miaow!

Yay!

Draw Woolly!

Follow the steps and count the legs.

  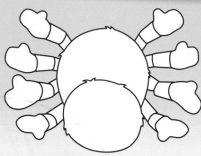 

1 First, draw **2 circles.**

2 Then add **8 legs.**

3 Draw **8** little **feet.**

4 Now draw Woolly's **face!**

Brilliant drawing!

Great job!

Opposites

Try these picture puzzles!

I'm Kit!

I'm Pup!

Is Kit **above** or **below** Pup?

above

below

Is Kit **inside** or **outside** the tent?

inside

outside

Is Pup **on** or **under** the picnic rug?

on

under

Is the tree **behind** or **in front** of Kit?

in front

behind

43

Number magic

Count along with the Numberblocks!

$6 + 1 = \boxed{}$ $7 + 1 = \boxed{}$

I'm Six!

I'm lucky number Seven!

Snack time!

Circle **6 apples** for Six!

Circle the group with **7 sandwiches.**

$8 + 1 =$ ⬜

$9 + 1 =$ ⬜

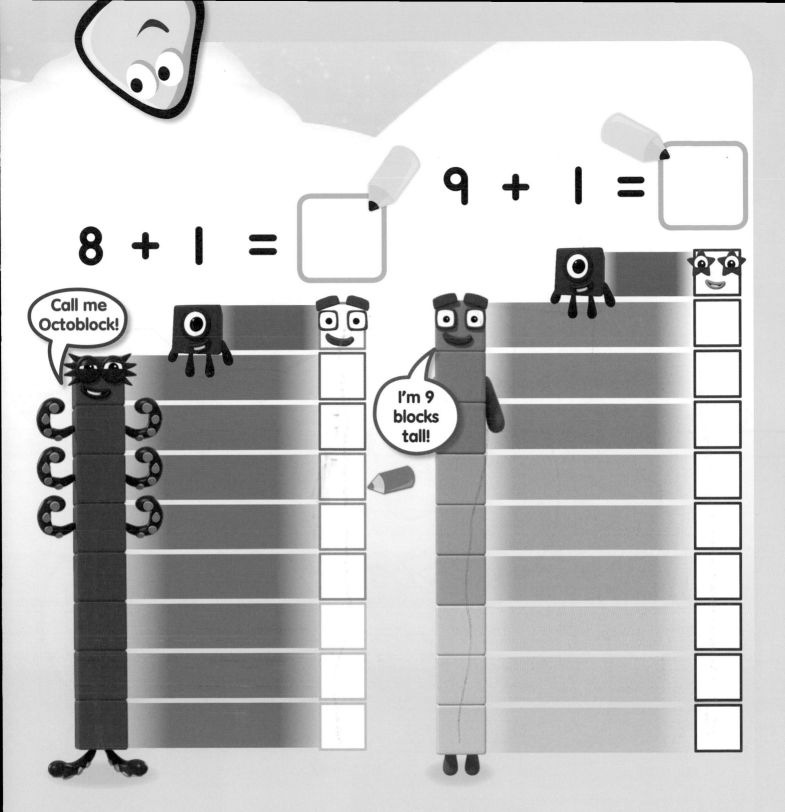

Call me Octoblock!

I'm 9 blocks tall!

Circle **8 bananas** for Eight!

Circle the group with **9 cupcakes**.

The Truckster

This vehicle takes the Go Jetters wherever they want to go!

Let's roll!

It has... awesome wheels!

It can even drive on water!

I love fixing the Truckster!

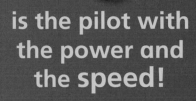 is the pilot with the power and the speed!

is fantastic when gymnastics are what you need!

can make and fix things super quickly with his hands.

can crack the answer to Grandmaster Glitch's plans!

47

Amazing maze

Read about Bitz and Bob's lost puppy.

One day, Bitz and Bob were in their treehouse. Bob was playing with Earl, the toy puppy. "Today is the opening of our **a-maze-ing MAZE!"** cheered Bitz, next to a maze of colourful blocks.

They closed their eyes… and suddenly the maze of blocks was real! Behind them was a giant hot-air balloon. "Wow!" gasped Bob, as Purl and Bevel raced over. Suddenly, Earl the puppy ran off, straight into the maze. **"Oh no, we've lost Earl!"** cried Bob.

Woof!

"Hmm, we need to be high up to spot Earl in the maze," said Bitz. "If only you could fly," sighed Bob. "Oh, but I can!" cheered Bitz and pointed to the hot-air balloon. "That's it! **Steam pink style!"** Bitz raced to the hot-air balloon and zoomed up high. "I can see you all and the whole maze, so I can direct you to Earl!" she called. "Let's go!" said Bob. "Go forward 3 blocks," cried Bitz. **"1, 2, 3," counted Bob.** "Turn right," said Bitz. The friends turned right.

Boo-yah!

"Now, go forward 2 blocks," called Bitz. **"1, 2," counted Purl.**

"You're nearly there," cried Bitz. The friends followed Bitz's directions until it led them to Earl the puppy! **"We found you!"** giggled Bob. "Woof!" woofed Earl. "Way to go, little bro!" called Bitz. "Boo-yah!" said Bevel.

Bitz helped the friends get out of the maze again. Soon enough the castle started to fade, the maze disappeared... and Bitz and Bob found themselves back in the treehouse. **"That was a-maze-ing!"** yawned Bob, snuggling up with Earl for a rest.

What an adventure!

That was brilliant!

Flying kites

The Furchester friends are having fun in the wind!

51

Pirate code

Help Gem solve the secret message!

I've lost my treasure map, but I've found a message in code.

= a	= b	= C	 = d
= e	= f	= g	 = h
= i	= j	 = k	= L
= m	= n	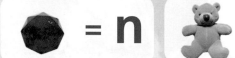 = o	 = p
= q	= r	= S	 = t
= u	= V	 = W	 = X
= y	 = z		

Ha ha, you'll never crack my secret code.

Use the Swashbuckle code to write out the secret message.

Who told Cook and Line to take the map?

✓ **Tick** your answer.

You're a star code-cracker!

53

Shapes

Draw and colour with Mr Tumble!

Can you find all the friends?

Hello!

Are you ready for another adventure?

✓ **Tick when you spot...**

Peter Rabbit	Cotton-tail	Jeremy Fisher	Pig Robinson	Squirrel Nutkin	Benjamin Bouncer	The Shrew

We'll get those rotten rabbits!

Quack! Quack!

Mr Tod	Mrs Bobtail	Lily Bobtail	Jemima Puddle-duck	Mrs Rabbit	Mr Bouncer	Old Brown

Charlie and Lola®

Cloud squiggles

Draw some fluffy cloud pictures with Charlie and Lola.

You could draw a **funny monster**, a **fluffy sheep** or something else.

Ooooh, funny clouds!

So fluffy!

59

Stripy tiger

Find out about this big cat!

Look what I've spotted in the jungle!

Super stripes

Every tiger has its own pattern of stripes. They **help it to hide** when hunting.

ROAR!

Pouncing paws

Tigers are great at jumping and have strong paws with sharp claws!

60

Great white shark

Meet a toothy creature!

SNAP!

Sharp teeth
The great white shark has **300** teeth.

Watch me whoosh!

I'm super speedy!

Speedy swimmer
It swims really fast!

Wow, the great white shark is huge!

Baking

Add some colour to Duggee's
kitchen and draw him a cake.

1 Use straight lines for the cupcake case and curvy ones for the icing.

2 Add a carrot to the top of your cake, like this.

3 Finish off with sprinkles and a stripy pattern for the cupcake case. Yummy!

Draw your cake here!

cake

Day and night

Find out about day and night with the twins.

day

In the **daytime,** you can see the sun...

...and clouds in the sky.

Colour a big, shining yellow sun.

During the day is when we play!

Who is playing on the slide?

Tim

or

Topsy

Bees come out in the daytime to find flowers.

Show the bee the way to the flowers.

night

Night-time is when the moon and the stars appear.

Draw around the moon.

Have you ever seen the moon in the sky?

At night, we snuggle up in bed.

Choose a toy for Topsy to cuddle in bed.

This one!

This one!

Listen to what sounds you can hear at bedtime tonight.

At night-time, **owls** come out and say...

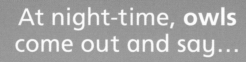
twit-twoo!

Tree fu spell

Try the helping hands spell.
Colour the leaves as you go.

66

1 Hold your **hands out** in front of you.

2 Slowly **bring your arms down** by your sides.

3 Put your left hand **behind your head.**

4 Now your **right hand!**

5 Stretch up with your left hand.

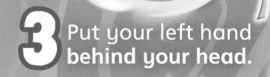

6 Now your **right hand!**

Odds and evens

Find out what makes an odd and an even number!

I'm odd! 1

I'm even! 2

I'm odd! 3

I'm even! 4

I'm odd! 5 — These odd Numberblocks have a block that sticks out on top!

Which Numberblock is the next odd number after 3?

3

5 or 2

Which Numberblock is the next even number after 2?

2

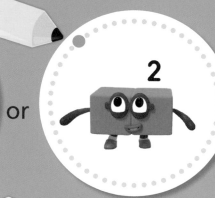

or 4

An even number can be split into two equal parts.

4

Which 2 Numberblocks make 4?

2 2

or

2 3

Star gazing

Clangers

Join the dots to draw what
the Clangers can see!

It's bedtime!

Get Waffle, Evie and Doug ready for bed.

Monster sleepover

Colour in this roarsome picture.

Bedtime story

It's time for a sleepover with Sarah & Duck!

When you see these pictures, say the names.

Sarah	Duck	John	Flamingo	Moon	Scooter Boy

 and were having a sleepover. Knock, knock! Someone was at the door. "Quack!" quacked and went to open it. It was . Soon, and arrived too. "Hello," said . "Let's play Same Bread Snap!" **The friends played until the sun set.** won every round. "She's good," said . "She likes to win," agreed .

They all brushed their teeth and washed their faces. Then covered her bed in a big blanket, rolled out his sleeping bag and popped up his tent. "Goodnight," yawned and shut her eyes. A little while later,  crawled out of his tent. "I can't sleep," he said, and all the friends woke up. **"How will we get to sleep now?"** sighed 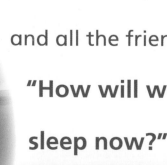.

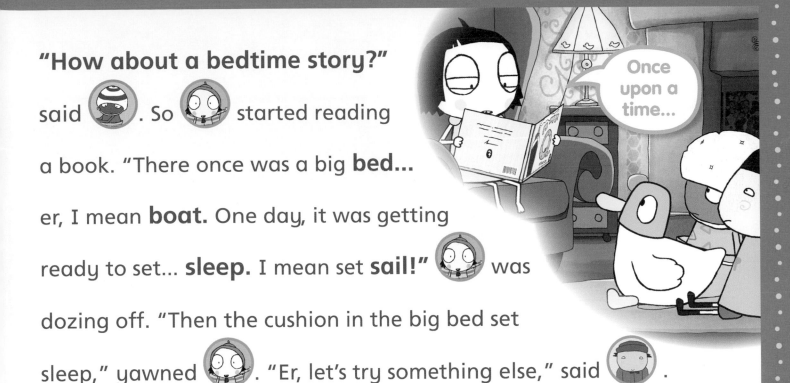

"How about a bedtime story?" said . So started reading a book. "There once was a big **bed...** er, I mean **boat.** One day, it was getting ready to set... **sleep.** I mean set **sail!**" was dozing off. "Then the cushion in the big bed set sleep," yawned . "Er, let's try something else," said .

Then spotted . "Maybe Moon can help!" said and ran over to her telescope. "Moon, how do you get to sleep?" asked .

"First, I do some big stretches. Then I brush each tooth. Sideways, upways and down," said . "Then I think about **slow things.** Like owls, because they blink rather slowly. Blink... blink... blink," said .

Then he noticed that his calm, soothing voice had sent , , , and **off to sleep.**

Well done, !

The end.

Once upon a time...

Zzzzzz!

75

Answers

Pages 8-9

Sula is holding the wand.

The **Brussels sprout** toy comes next.

There are **more orange balloons**.

There are **5** balloons in total.

Pages 22-23

There are **5** rubber ducks.

Pages 32-33

Pages 34-35

a	l	o	g
b	e	e	a
u	n	e	n
g	p	n	t

Pages 36-37

There are **7** spots on the little ladybird.

Page 43

Pages 44-45

The answers to the Numberblocks sums are:

$$6 + 1 = 7$$

$$7 + 1 = 8$$

$$8 + 1 = 9$$

$$9 + 1 = 10$$

The answers to the puzzles are:

Circle **6 apples** for Six!

Circle the group with **7 sandwiches**.

Circle **8 bananas** for Eight!

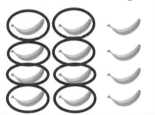

Circle the group with **9 cupcakes**.

Pages 46-47

The Truckster has **6** wheels.

1   2   3   4   5   6

Pages 56-57

Pages 52-53

Cook and Line have taken the map

Captain

Captain

Page 68

The odd Numberblock that comes next is **5**.

The even Numberblock that comes next is **4**.

The two even Numberblocks that make **4** are **2** and **2**.